Everything You Ever Want

Everything You Ever Wanted to Know About…

Everything You Ever Wanted to Know About…

Everything You Ever Wanted to Know About…

Everything You Ever Wanted to Know About…

Everything You Ever Wanted to Know About…

Everything You Ever Wanted to Know About…

Everything You Ever Wanted to Know About…

Everything You Ever Wanted to Know About…

Everything You Ever Wanted to Know About…

Everything You Ever Wanted to Know About…

Everything You Ever Wanted to Know About…

Everything You Ever Wanted to Know About…

Everything You Ever Wanted to Know About…

Everything You Ever Wanted to Know About…

Everything You Ever Wanted to Know About…

Everything You Ever Wanted to Know About…

Everything You Ever Wanted to Know About…

Everything You Ever Wanted to Know About…

Everything You Ever Wanted to Know About…

Everything You Ever Wanted to Know About…

Everything You Ever Wanted to Know About...

Everything You Ever Wanted to Know About…

Everything You Ever Wanted to Know About…

Everything You Ever Wanted to Know About…

Everything You Ever Wanted to Know About…

Everything You Ever Wanted to Know About…

Everything You Ever Wanted to Know About…

Everything You Ever Wanted to Know About…

Everything You Ever Wanted to Know About…

Everything You Ever Wanted to Know About…

Everything You Ever Wanted to Know About…

Everything You Ever Wanted to Know About…

Everything You Ever Wanted to Know About…

Everything You Ever Wanted to Know About…

Everything You Ever Wanted to Know About…

Everything You Ever Wanted to Know About…

Everything You Ever Wanted to Know About…

Everything You Ever Wanted to Know About…

Everything You Ever Wanted to Know About…

Everything You Ever Wanted to Know About…

Everything You Ever Wanted to Know About…

Everything You Ever Wanted to Know About…

Everything You Ever Wanted to Know About…

Everything You Ever Wanted to Know About…

Everything You Ever Wanted to Know About…

Everything You Ever Wanted to Know About…

Everything You Ever Wanted to Know About…

Everything You Ever Wanted to Know About…

Everything You Ever Wanted to Know About…

Everything You Ever Wanted to Know About…

Everything You Ever Wanted to Know About…

Everything You Ever Wanted to Know About…

Everything You Ever Wanted to Know About…

Everything You Ever Wanted to Know About…

Everything You Ever Wanted to Know About…

Everything You Ever Wanted to Know About…

Everything You Ever Wanted to Know About…

Everything You Ever Wanted to Know About…

Everything You Ever Wanted to Know About…

Everything You Ever Wanted to Know About…

Everything You Ever Wanted to Know About…

Everything You Ever Wanted to Know About…

Everything You Ever Wanted to Know About…

Everything You Ever Wanted to Know About…

Everything You Ever Wanted to Know About…

Everything You Ever Wanted to Know About…

Everything You Ever Wanted to Know About…

Everything You Ever Wanted to Know About…

Everything You Ever Wanted to Know About…

Everything You Ever Wanted to Know About…

Everything You Ever Wanted to Know About…

Everything You Ever Wanted to Know About…

Everything You Ever Wanted to Know About…

Everything You Ever Wanted to Know About…

Everything You Ever Wanted to Know About…

Everything You Ever Wanted to Know About…

Everything You Ever Wanted to Know About…

Everything You Ever Wanted to Know About…

Everything You Ever Wanted to Know About…

Everything You Ever Wanted to Know About…

Everything You Ever Wanted to Know About…

Everything You Ever Wanted to Know About…

Everything You Ever Wanted to Know About…

Everything You Ever Wanted to Know About…

Everything You Ever Wanted to Know About…

Everything You Ever Wanted to Know About…

Everything You Ever Wanted to Know About…

Everything You Ever Wanted to Know About…

Everything You Ever Wanted to Know About…

Everything You Ever Wanted to Know About…

Everything You Ever Wanted to Know About…

Everything You Ever Wanted to Know About…

Everything You Ever Wanted to Know About…

Everything You Ever Wanted to Know About…

Everything You Ever Wanted to Know About…

Everything You Ever Wanted to Know About…

Everything You Ever Wanted to Know About…

Everything You Ever Wanted to Know About…

Everything You Ever Wanted to Know About…

Everything You Ever Wanted to Know About…

Everything You Ever Wanted to Know About…

Everything You Ever Wanted to Know About…

Everything You Ever Wanted to Know About…

Everything You Ever Wanted to Know About…

Everything You Ever Wanted to Know About…

Everything You Ever Wanted to Know About…

Everything You Ever Wanted to Know About…

Everything You Ever Wanted to Know About…

Everything You Ever Wanted to Know About…

Everything You Ever Wanted to Know About…

Everything You Ever Wanted to Know About…

Everything You Ever Wanted to Know About…

Everything You Ever Wanted to Know About…

Everything You Ever Wanted to Know About…

Everything You Ever Wanted to Know About…

Everything You Ever Wanted to Know About…

Everything You Ever Wanted to Know About…

Everything You Ever Wanted to Know About…

Everything You Ever Wanted to Know About…

Everything You Ever Wanted to Know About…

Everything You Ever Wanted to Know About…

Everything You Ever Wanted to Know About…

Everything You Ever Wanted to Know About…

Everything You Ever Wanted to Know About…

Everything You Ever Wanted to Know About…

Everything You Ever Wanted to Know About…

Everything You Ever Wanted to Know About…

Everything You Ever Wanted to Know About…

Everything You Ever Wanted to Know About…

Everything You Ever Wanted to Know About…

Everything You Ever Wanted to Know About…

Everything You Ever Wanted to Know About…

Printed in Great Britain
by Amazon